50 Meals in a Mug
Recipes for Home

By: Kelly Johnson

Table of Contents

- Mug Mac and Cheese
- Cheesy Broccoli Rice
- Chicken Alfredo Pasta
- Mug Pizza
- Vegetable Fried Rice
- Breakfast Omelette
- Chocolate Chip Cookie
- Mug Quiche
- Savory Oatmeal
- Spaghetti Aglio e Olio
- Beef Stroganoff
- Caprese Salad
- Curry Lentil Soup
- Mug Lasagna
- Taco Rice Bowl
- Greek Yogurt Parfait
- Apple Crisp
- Egg and Spinach Mug
- Peanut Butter Banana Oatmeal
- Chili in a Mug
- Veggie Quinoa Bowl
- Banana Bread
- Chocolate Lava Cake
- Shrimp Fried Rice
- Creamy Tomato Soup
- Chicken and Rice Casserole
- Teriyaki Salmon Bowl
- Sweet Potato Mash
- Veggie Burrito Bowl
- Instant Ramen with Egg
- Cinnamon Roll
- Muffin in a Mug
- Breakfast Burrito
- S'mores Mug Cake
- Thai Peanut Noodles

- Mediterranean Couscous
- Stuffed Bell Pepper
- Tuna Salad
- Coconut Curry Soup
- Pesto Pasta
- Veggie Stir-Fry
- Chocolate Mousse
- Honey Garlic Chicken
- Apple Cinnamon Oatmeal
- Pumpkin Spice Mug Cake
- Beef and Broccoli
- Frittata with Veggies
- Spinach and Feta Rice
- Raspberry Almond Mug Cake
- Nacho Cheese Dip

Mug Mac and Cheese

Ingredients:

- 1/2 cup elbow macaroni
- 1/2 cup water
- 1/4 cup milk
- 1/2 cup shredded cheddar cheese
- Salt and pepper to taste
- Optional: garlic powder or paprika

Instructions:

1. **Cook the Pasta:**
    - Combine macaroni and water in a microwave-safe mug. Microwave on high for 2-3 minutes, stirring halfway.
2. **Add Milk and Cheese:**
    - Stir in milk and cheese until combined.
3. **Microwave Again:**
    - Heat for another 30-60 seconds until cheese is melted.
4. **Season:**
    - Add salt, pepper, and any optional seasonings.
5. **Enjoy:**
    - Let cool slightly before eating. Customize with add-ins if desired!

Cheesy Broccoli Rice

Ingredients:

- 1 cup cooked rice
- 1 cup broccoli florets (fresh or frozen)
- 1/2 cup shredded cheddar cheese
- 1/4 cup milk
- Salt and pepper to taste

Instructions:

1. **Cook Broccoli:** Steam or microwave broccoli until tender.
2. **Combine:** In a bowl, mix cooked rice, broccoli, milk, cheese, salt, and pepper.
3. **Heat:** Microwave for 1-2 minutes until heated through and cheese is melted. Stir well and enjoy!

Chicken Alfredo Pasta

Ingredients:

- 1 cup cooked pasta (fettuccine or your choice)
- 1/2 cup cooked chicken (shredded or diced)
- 1/4 cup heavy cream
- 1/2 cup grated Parmesan cheese
- Salt and pepper to taste

Instructions:

1. **Mix:** In a bowl, combine cooked pasta, chicken, heavy cream, and Parmesan.
2. **Heat:** Microwave for 1-2 minutes until heated through.
3. **Season:** Stir well, add salt and pepper, and enjoy your creamy dish!

Mug Pizza

Ingredients:

- 4 tablespoons all-purpose flour
- 1/8 teaspoon baking powder
- 1/8 teaspoon salt
- 3 tablespoons milk
- 1 tablespoon olive oil
- 2 tablespoons pizza sauce
- 1/4 cup shredded mozzarella cheese
- Toppings of choice (pepperoni, veggies, etc.)

Instructions:

1. **Mix Dry Ingredients:** In a microwave-safe mug, combine flour, baking powder, and salt.
2. **Add Wet Ingredients:** Stir in milk and olive oil until smooth.
3. **Layer:** Add pizza sauce, cheese, and toppings on top.
4. **Microwave:** Heat for 1-2 minutes until the dough rises and cheese is melted. Let cool slightly before enjoying!

Feel free to customize each recipe to your taste!

Vegetable Fried Rice

Ingredients:

- 2 cups cooked rice
- 1 cup mixed vegetables (frozen or fresh)
- 2 tablespoons soy sauce
- 1 tablespoon sesame oil
- 2 green onions, chopped
- Salt and pepper to taste

Instructions:

1. **Sauté Veggies:** In a pan, heat sesame oil and sauté mixed vegetables until tender.
2. **Add Rice:** Stir in the cooked rice and soy sauce, mixing well.
3. **Finish:** Cook for a few minutes, then add green onions and season to taste.

Breakfast Omelette

Ingredients:

- 2 eggs
- 2 tablespoons milk
- Salt and pepper to taste
- 1/4 cup diced vegetables (bell peppers, onions, spinach)
- 1/4 cup shredded cheese

Instructions:

1. **Whisk Eggs:** In a bowl, whisk together eggs, milk, salt, and pepper.
2. **Cook:** Pour into a heated pan and add vegetables. Cook until set.
3. **Add Cheese:** Sprinkle cheese on top, fold, and serve once melted.

Chocolate Chip Cookie

Ingredients:

- 1/2 cup softened butter
- 1/4 cup sugar
- 1/4 cup brown sugar
- 1/2 teaspoon vanilla extract
- 1 egg
- 1 cup flour
- 1/2 teaspoon baking soda
- 1/2 cup chocolate chips

Instructions:

1. **Mix Wet Ingredients:** Cream butter and sugars, then add vanilla and egg.
2. **Combine Dry Ingredients:** Mix flour and baking soda, then combine with wet ingredients.
3. **Add Chips:** Stir in chocolate chips and bake at 350°F (175°C) for 10-12 minutes.

Mug Quiche

Ingredients:

- 2 eggs
- 2 tablespoons milk
- 1/4 cup diced vegetables
- 2 tablespoons shredded cheese
- Salt and pepper to taste

Instructions:

1. **Mix Ingredients:** In a microwave-safe mug, whisk eggs, milk, salt, and pepper. Stir in vegetables and cheese.
2. **Microwave:** Cook for 1-2 minutes until the eggs are set. Let cool slightly before enjoying.

Savory Oatmeal

Ingredients:

- 1 cup water or broth
- 1/2 cup rolled oats
- 1/4 cup sautéed vegetables (spinach, mushrooms, etc.)
- 1/4 cup shredded cheese
- Salt and pepper to taste

Instructions:

1. **Cook Oats:** In a pot, bring water or broth to a boil, then add oats. Cook until tender.
2. **Combine:** Stir in sautéed vegetables, cheese, salt, and pepper.

Spaghetti Aglio e Olio

Ingredients:

- 8 ounces spaghetti
- 4 cloves garlic, sliced
- 1/2 teaspoon red pepper flakes
- 1/4 cup olive oil
- Parsley, chopped
- Salt to taste

Instructions:

1. **Cook Pasta:** Boil spaghetti until al dente, then drain.
2. **Sauté Garlic:** In a pan, heat olive oil and sauté garlic and red pepper flakes.
3. **Combine:** Toss spaghetti with garlic oil and parsley. Season with salt.

Beef Stroganoff

Ingredients:

- 1 pound beef, sliced
- 1 onion, chopped
- 2 cups mushrooms, sliced
- 1 cup beef broth
- 1/2 cup sour cream
- Salt and pepper to taste
- Cooked noodles for serving

Instructions:

1. **Cook Beef:** In a skillet, brown beef, then add onions and mushrooms.
2. **Simmer:** Add broth, simmer until tender, then stir in sour cream. Season to taste.
3. **Serve:** Pour over cooked noodles.

Caprese Salad

Ingredients:

- 2 large tomatoes, sliced
- 8 ounces fresh mozzarella, sliced
- Fresh basil leaves
- Olive oil
- Balsamic vinegar
- Salt and pepper to taste

Instructions:

1. **Layer Ingredients:** Alternate layers of tomatoes, mozzarella, and basil on a plate.
2. **Drizzle:** Drizzle with olive oil and balsamic vinegar, then season with salt and pepper.

Enjoy these delicious recipes!

Curry Lentil Soup

Ingredients:

- 1 cup lentils (rinsed)
- 1 onion, diced
- 2 carrots, diced
- 2 garlic cloves, minced
- 1 tablespoon curry powder
- 4 cups vegetable broth
- 1 can coconut milk
- Salt and pepper to taste
- Fresh cilantro (optional)

Instructions:

1. **Sauté Vegetables:** In a pot, sauté onion, carrots, and garlic until soft.
2. **Add Ingredients:** Stir in lentils, curry powder, broth, and coconut milk. Bring to a boil.
3. **Simmer:** Reduce heat and simmer for 25-30 minutes until lentils are tender. Season to taste. Garnish with cilantro if desired.

Mug Lasagna

Ingredients:

- 1/2 cup cooked pasta (lasagna noodles, broken)
- 1/4 cup marinara sauce
- 1/4 cup ricotta cheese
- 1/4 cup shredded mozzarella cheese
- 1 tablespoon grated Parmesan cheese
- Italian seasoning to taste

Instructions:

1. **Layer Ingredients:** In a microwave-safe mug, layer pasta, marinara, ricotta, mozzarella, and Italian seasoning.
2. **Repeat Layers:** Repeat layers until ingredients are used up.
3. **Microwave:** Cook for 2-3 minutes until heated through and cheese is melted. Let cool slightly before eating.

Taco Rice Bowl

Ingredients:

- 1 cup cooked rice
- 1/2 cup cooked ground beef or turkey (seasoned with taco seasoning)
- 1/4 cup black beans (drained and rinsed)
- 1/4 cup corn
- 1/4 cup salsa
- Shredded cheese, avocado, and cilantro for topping

Instructions:

1. **Combine Ingredients:** In a bowl, mix rice, meat, beans, corn, and salsa.
2. **Heat:** Microwave for 1-2 minutes until warm.
3. **Serve:** Top with cheese, avocado, and cilantro.

Greek Yogurt Parfait

Ingredients:

- 1 cup Greek yogurt
- 1/2 cup granola
- 1 cup mixed berries (strawberries, blueberries, etc.)
- Honey (optional)

Instructions:

1. **Layer Ingredients:** In a glass or bowl, layer Greek yogurt, granola, and berries.
2. **Drizzle Honey:** If desired, drizzle with honey between layers.
3. **Serve:** Enjoy immediately!

Apple Crisp

Ingredients:

- 2 apples, peeled and sliced
- 1/2 cup oats
- 1/4 cup brown sugar
- 1/4 cup flour
- 1/4 teaspoon cinnamon
- 2 tablespoons butter, melted

Instructions:

1. **Preheat Oven:** Preheat oven to 350°F (175°C).
2. **Mix Topping:** In a bowl, combine oats, brown sugar, flour, cinnamon, and melted butter.
3. **Layer Apples:** Place sliced apples in a baking dish and sprinkle the topping over them.
4. **Bake:** Bake for 25-30 minutes until apples are tender and topping is golden.

Egg and Spinach Mug

Ingredients:

- 2 eggs
- 1/2 cup fresh spinach (chopped)
- 2 tablespoons milk
- Salt and pepper to taste
- Grated cheese (optional)

Instructions:

1. **Mix Ingredients:** In a microwave-safe mug, whisk eggs, milk, spinach, salt, and pepper.
2. **Microwave:** Cook for 1-2 minutes until eggs are set. Stir halfway through.
3. **Add Cheese:** If desired, sprinkle cheese on top and microwave for another 30 seconds.

Peanut Butter Banana Oatmeal

Ingredients:

- 1/2 cup rolled oats
- 1 cup milk or water
- 1 banana (sliced)
- 2 tablespoons peanut butter
- Honey or maple syrup (optional)

Instructions:

1. **Cook Oats:** In a pot, bring milk or water to a boil. Add oats and reduce heat. Cook until tender.
2. **Combine:** Stir in sliced banana and peanut butter.
3. **Sweeten:** Drizzle with honey or syrup if desired.

Chili in a Mug

Ingredients:

- 1 cup cooked ground beef or turkey
- 1 can (15 oz) kidney beans (drained and rinsed)
- 1 can (15 oz) diced tomatoes
- 1 tablespoon chili powder
- Salt and pepper to taste

Instructions:

1. **Combine Ingredients:** In a microwave-safe mug, mix meat, beans, tomatoes, chili powder, salt, and pepper.
2. **Microwave:** Heat for 2-3 minutes until hot, stirring halfway through.
3. **Serve:** Enjoy your quick chili!

Feel free to customize these recipes to suit your taste!

Veggie Quinoa Bowl

Ingredients:

- 1 cup cooked quinoa
- 1 cup mixed vegetables (bell peppers, zucchini, carrots)
- 1/2 cup chickpeas (drained and rinsed)
- 2 tablespoons olive oil
- Juice of 1 lemon
- Salt and pepper to taste
- Fresh herbs (parsley or cilantro) for garnish

Instructions:

1. **Sauté Vegetables:** In a pan, heat olive oil and sauté mixed vegetables until tender.
2. **Combine:** In a bowl, mix quinoa, sautéed veggies, and chickpeas. Drizzle with lemon juice, and season with salt and pepper.
3. **Garnish:** Top with fresh herbs and enjoy!

Banana Bread

Ingredients:

- 3 ripe bananas (mashed)
- 1/3 cup melted butter
- 1 teaspoon baking soda
- Pinch of salt
- 3/4 cup sugar
- 1 large egg (beaten)
- 1 teaspoon vanilla extract
- 1 cup flour

Instructions:

1. **Preheat Oven:** Preheat oven to 350°F (175°C).
2. **Mix Ingredients:** In a bowl, mix mashed bananas with melted butter. Stir in baking soda and salt. Add sugar, egg, and vanilla. Mix in flour.
3. **Bake:** Pour into a greased loaf pan and bake for 60-65 minutes, or until a toothpick comes out clean.

Chocolate Lava Cake

Ingredients:

- 1/2 cup unsalted butter
- 1 cup chocolate chips
- 2 eggs
- 2 egg yolks
- 1/4 cup sugar
- 2 tablespoons flour

Instructions:

1. **Preheat Oven:** Preheat oven to 425°F (220°C).
2. **Melt Chocolate:** In a microwave-safe bowl, melt butter and chocolate chips together until smooth.
3. **Mix:** In another bowl, whisk eggs, egg yolks, and sugar. Gradually add chocolate mixture, then fold in flour.
4. **Bake:** Pour into greased ramekins and bake for 12-14 minutes until edges are firm but center is soft. Let cool slightly before serving.

Shrimp Fried Rice

Ingredients:

- 2 cups cooked rice
- 1 cup shrimp (peeled and deveined)
- 1 cup mixed vegetables (peas, carrots)
- 2 tablespoons soy sauce
- 1 tablespoon sesame oil
- 2 green onions, chopped
- Salt and pepper to taste

Instructions:

1. **Cook Shrimp:** In a pan, heat sesame oil and sauté shrimp until cooked through. Remove and set aside.
2. **Sauté Veggies:** In the same pan, add mixed vegetables and cook until tender. Add rice and soy sauce.
3. **Combine:** Stir in shrimp and green onions. Cook until heated through. Season with salt and pepper.

Creamy Tomato Soup

Ingredients:

- 1 can (28 oz) crushed tomatoes
- 1 cup vegetable broth
- 1/2 cup heavy cream
- 1 onion (chopped)
- 2 garlic cloves (minced)
- 1 tablespoon olive oil
- Salt and pepper to taste
- Fresh basil for garnish

Instructions:

1. **Sauté Onion and Garlic:** In a pot, heat olive oil and sauté onion and garlic until soft.
2. **Add Tomatoes and Broth:** Stir in crushed tomatoes and vegetable broth. Simmer for 15 minutes.
3. **Blend:** Remove from heat, add cream, and blend until smooth. Season with salt and pepper. Garnish with fresh basil.

Chicken and Rice Casserole

Ingredients:

- 2 cups cooked rice
- 2 cups cooked chicken (shredded)
- 1 can (10.5 oz) cream of chicken soup
- 1 cup frozen mixed vegetables
- 1 cup shredded cheese
- Salt and pepper to taste

Instructions:

1. **Preheat Oven:** Preheat oven to 350°F (175°C).
2. **Combine Ingredients:** In a large bowl, mix rice, chicken, cream of chicken soup, vegetables, and half the cheese. Season with salt and pepper.
3. **Bake:** Pour into a greased baking dish, top with remaining cheese, and bake for 25-30 minutes until bubbly.

Teriyaki Salmon Bowl

Ingredients:

- 2 salmon fillets
- 1/4 cup teriyaki sauce
- 2 cups cooked rice
- 1 cup steamed broccoli
- Sesame seeds for garnish

Instructions:

1. **Marinate Salmon:** Marinate salmon fillets in teriyaki sauce for at least 15 minutes.
2. **Cook Salmon:** Grill or bake salmon at 400°F (200°C) for 12-15 minutes, basting with marinade.
3. **Assemble Bowl:** Serve salmon over rice, topped with steamed broccoli and sesame seeds.

Sweet Potato Mash

Ingredients:

- 2 large sweet potatoes (peeled and cubed)
- 1/4 cup milk (or cream)
- 2 tablespoons butter
- Salt and pepper to taste

Instructions:

1. **Boil Sweet Potatoes:** Boil sweet potatoes until tender, about 15-20 minutes. Drain.
2. **Mash:** In a bowl, mash sweet potatoes with milk, butter, salt, and pepper until smooth.
3. **Serve:** Enjoy as a side dish!

Feel free to adjust these recipes to your taste!

Veggie Burrito Bowl

Ingredients:

- 1 cup cooked rice or quinoa
- 1/2 cup black beans (drained and rinsed)
- 1/2 cup corn (canned or frozen)
- 1/2 cup diced tomatoes
- 1/2 avocado (sliced)
- 1/4 cup salsa
- 1 tablespoon lime juice
- Fresh cilantro for garnish

Instructions:

1. **Combine Base:** In a bowl, start with cooked rice or quinoa.
2. **Layer Ingredients:** Top with black beans, corn, diced tomatoes, and avocado.
3. **Add Salsa:** Drizzle salsa and lime juice over the top. Garnish with fresh cilantro and enjoy!

Instant Ramen with Egg

Ingredients:

- 1 package instant ramen noodles
- 2 cups water
- 1 egg
- Green onions (sliced, optional)
- Soy sauce or sriracha (optional)

Instructions:

1. **Cook Noodles:** In a pot, bring water to a boil. Add ramen noodles and cook according to package instructions.
2. **Add Egg:** Crack the egg into the pot in the last minute of cooking and stir gently to create ribbons.
3. **Season:** Remove from heat, add seasoning packet, and stir. Top with green onions and drizzle with soy sauce or sriracha if desired.

Cinnamon Roll

Ingredients:

- 1 cup flour
- 1/2 tablespoon baking powder
- 1/4 teaspoon salt
- 1 tablespoon sugar
- 1/2 cup milk
- 2 tablespoons melted butter
- 1 tablespoon cinnamon
- 2 tablespoons brown sugar

Instructions:

1. **Mix Dry Ingredients:** In a bowl, mix flour, baking powder, salt, and sugar.
2. **Add Wet Ingredients:** Stir in milk and melted butter until combined.
3. **Add Filling:** Roll out the dough, spread with butter, sprinkle with cinnamon and brown sugar, and roll up tightly. Slice into rounds.
4. **Bake:** Place in a greased baking dish and bake at 350°F (175°C) for 15-20 minutes until golden.

Muffin in a Mug

Ingredients:

- 4 tablespoons flour
- 1/4 teaspoon baking powder
- 1 tablespoon sugar
- 1 tablespoon milk
- 1 tablespoon vegetable oil
- Optional add-ins: chocolate chips, blueberries, or nuts

Instructions:

1. **Mix Ingredients:** In a microwave-safe mug, mix flour, baking powder, and sugar. Add milk and oil, and stir until combined. Fold in any optional add-ins.
2. **Microwave:** Cook in the microwave for about 1-2 minutes until the muffin rises and is cooked through.
3. **Cool:** Let cool slightly before enjoying.

Breakfast Burrito

Ingredients:

- 2 eggs
- 1/4 cup cooked sausage or bacon (optional)
- 1/4 cup shredded cheese
- 1 tortilla
- Salsa (optional)

Instructions:

1. **Scramble Eggs:** In a bowl, whisk eggs and scramble them in a pan until cooked.
2. **Assemble Burrito:** Place scrambled eggs, meat (if using), and cheese on a tortilla. Add salsa if desired.
3. **Wrap:** Roll the tortilla tightly, then heat in the pan for a minute on each side to crisp it up.

S'mores Mug Cake

Ingredients:

- 4 tablespoons flour
- 2 tablespoons sugar
- 1/8 teaspoon baking powder
- 3 tablespoons milk
- 1 tablespoon melted butter
- 2 tablespoons chocolate chips
- 2 marshmallows

Instructions:

1. **Mix Ingredients:** In a microwave-safe mug, combine flour, sugar, and baking powder. Stir in milk and melted butter until smooth. Fold in chocolate chips.
2. **Add Marshmallows:** Place marshmallows on top of the batter.
3. **Microwave:** Cook in the microwave for about 1-1.5 minutes until the cake rises. Let cool slightly before enjoying.

Thai Peanut Noodles

Ingredients:

- 8 oz noodles (rice or spaghetti)
- 1/4 cup peanut butter
- 2 tablespoons soy sauce
- 1 tablespoon honey or maple syrup
- 1 tablespoon lime juice
- 1/2 cup shredded carrots
- 1/2 cup sliced bell peppers
- Chopped peanuts and cilantro for garnish

Instructions:

1. **Cook Noodles:** Prepare noodles according to package instructions, then drain.
2. **Make Sauce:** In a bowl, mix peanut butter, soy sauce, honey, and lime juice until smooth.
3. **Combine:** Toss cooked noodles with sauce, shredded carrots, and bell peppers. Garnish with chopped peanuts and cilantro.

Mediterranean Couscous

Ingredients:

- 1 cup couscous
- 1 1/4 cups vegetable broth or water
- 1/2 cup cherry tomatoes (halved)
- 1/2 cucumber (diced)
- 1/4 cup feta cheese (crumbled)
- 2 tablespoons olive oil
- Juice of 1 lemon
- Salt and pepper to taste

Instructions:

1. **Cook Couscous:** In a pot, bring vegetable broth to a boil. Stir in couscous, cover, and remove from heat. Let sit for 5 minutes, then fluff with a fork.
2. **Mix Salad:** In a bowl, combine cooked couscous, tomatoes, cucumber, feta, olive oil, lemon juice, salt, and pepper.
3. **Serve:** Enjoy chilled or at room temperature.

Feel free to customize these recipes to suit your taste!

Stuffed Bell Pepper

Ingredients:

- 4 bell peppers (any color)
- 1 cup cooked rice (or quinoa)
- 1 can black beans (drained and rinsed)
- 1 cup corn (frozen or canned)
- 1 cup salsa
- 1 teaspoon cumin
- 1 cup shredded cheese

Instructions:

1. **Preheat Oven:** Preheat oven to 375°F (190°C).
2. **Prepare Peppers:** Cut the tops off the bell peppers and remove seeds.
3. **Mix Filling:** In a bowl, combine cooked rice, black beans, corn, salsa, and cumin.
4. **Stuff Peppers:** Fill each bell pepper with the mixture and place in a baking dish. Top with cheese.
5. **Bake:** Cover with foil and bake for 25 minutes. Remove foil and bake for an additional 10 minutes until cheese is bubbly.

Tuna Salad

Ingredients:

- 1 can tuna (drained)
- 1/4 cup mayonnaise
- 1 tablespoon Dijon mustard
- 1/4 cup celery (diced)
- 1/4 cup red onion (diced)
- Salt and pepper to taste
- Lettuce leaves or crackers for serving

Instructions:

1. **Mix Ingredients:** In a bowl, combine tuna, mayonnaise, Dijon mustard, celery, red onion, salt, and pepper.
2. **Serve:** Enjoy on lettuce leaves or with crackers.

Coconut Curry Soup

Ingredients:

- 1 can coconut milk
- 2 cups vegetable broth
- 1 tablespoon red curry paste
- 1 cup mixed vegetables (carrots, bell peppers, etc.)
- 1 cup cooked protein (tofu, chicken, or shrimp)
- Fresh cilantro for garnish

Instructions:

1. **Combine Ingredients:** In a pot, mix coconut milk, vegetable broth, and red curry paste. Bring to a simmer.
2. **Add Veggies and Protein:** Stir in mixed vegetables and cooked protein. Simmer for 10 minutes until heated through.
3. **Serve:** Garnish with fresh cilantro before serving.

Pesto Pasta

Ingredients:

- 8 oz pasta (your choice)
- 1/2 cup pesto (store-bought or homemade)
- 1/2 cup cherry tomatoes (halved)
- 1/4 cup grated Parmesan cheese
- Salt and pepper to taste

Instructions:

1. **Cook Pasta:** Boil pasta according to package instructions. Drain and reserve some pasta water.
2. **Mix with Pesto:** In a large bowl, combine pasta with pesto and cherry tomatoes. If needed, add a splash of reserved pasta water for creaminess.
3. **Serve:** Top with grated Parmesan and season with salt and pepper.

Veggie Stir-Fry

Ingredients:

- 2 cups mixed vegetables (broccoli, bell peppers, carrots, etc.)
- 1 tablespoon vegetable oil
- 2 tablespoons soy sauce
- 1 teaspoon ginger (grated)
- 1 teaspoon garlic (minced)
- Cooked rice or noodles for serving

Instructions:

1. **Heat Oil:** In a pan, heat vegetable oil over medium-high heat.
2. **Stir-Fry Veggies:** Add mixed vegetables, ginger, and garlic. Stir-fry for 5-7 minutes until tender.
3. **Add Sauce:** Stir in soy sauce and cook for another minute. Serve over rice or noodles.

Chocolate Mousse

Ingredients:

- 4 oz dark chocolate (chopped)
- 2 tablespoons butter
- 2 eggs (separated)
- 1/4 cup sugar
- 1/2 cup heavy cream

Instructions:

1. **Melt Chocolate:** In a bowl, melt chocolate and butter together in the microwave or over a double boiler.
2. **Whisk Eggs:** In a separate bowl, whisk egg yolks and sugar until pale and creamy. Gradually mix in the melted chocolate.
3. **Beat Egg Whites:** In another bowl, beat egg whites until stiff peaks form. Fold into the chocolate mixture.
4. **Whip Cream:** In a separate bowl, whip heavy cream until soft peaks form, then fold into the mixture.
5. **Chill:** Spoon into serving dishes and refrigerate for at least 2 hours before serving.

Honey Garlic Chicken

Ingredients:

- 1 lb chicken thighs (boneless, skinless)
- 1/4 cup honey
- 1/4 cup soy sauce
- 2 garlic cloves (minced)
- 1 tablespoon olive oil
- Sesame seeds and green onions for garnish

Instructions:

1. **Marinate Chicken:** In a bowl, mix honey, soy sauce, garlic, and olive oil. Add chicken and marinate for at least 30 minutes.
2. **Cook Chicken:** Heat a pan over medium heat. Cook chicken for about 5-7 minutes on each side until cooked through.
3. **Glaze:** Pour remaining marinade into the pan and simmer for a few minutes until thickened. Garnish with sesame seeds and green onions.

Apple Cinnamon Oatmeal

Ingredients:

- 1 cup rolled oats
- 2 cups water or milk
- 1 apple (diced)
- 1 teaspoon cinnamon
- 2 tablespoons brown sugar or honey
- Nuts or raisins for topping (optional)

Instructions:

1. **Cook Oats:** In a pot, bring water or milk to a boil. Stir in oats, diced apple, cinnamon, and brown sugar.
2. **Simmer:** Reduce heat and simmer for about 5 minutes until the oats are cooked and the mixture is thickened.
3. **Serve:** Top with nuts or raisins if desired.

Feel free to adjust these recipes to your taste! Enjoy!

Pumpkin Spice Mug Cake

Ingredients:

- 4 tablespoons flour
- 2 tablespoons sugar
- 1/4 teaspoon baking powder
- 1/4 teaspoon pumpkin pie spice
- 3 tablespoons milk
- 1 tablespoon vegetable oil
- 2 tablespoons pumpkin puree

Instructions:

1. **Mix Dry Ingredients:** In a microwave-safe mug, combine flour, sugar, baking powder, and pumpkin pie spice.
2. **Add Wet Ingredients:** Stir in milk, vegetable oil, and pumpkin puree until smooth.
3. **Microwave:** Cook for about 1-1.5 minutes until the cake has risen and is cooked through. Let cool slightly before enjoying.

Beef and Broccoli

Ingredients:

- 1 lb beef (sliced thin)
- 2 cups broccoli florets
- 1/4 cup soy sauce
- 2 tablespoons oyster sauce
- 2 tablespoons cornstarch
- 2 tablespoons vegetable oil
- 2 garlic cloves (minced)

Instructions:

1. **Marinate Beef:** In a bowl, combine beef with soy sauce and cornstarch. Let sit for 15 minutes.
2. **Cook Beef:** Heat oil in a pan and stir-fry beef until browned. Remove and set aside.
3. **Stir-Fry Broccoli:** In the same pan, add garlic and broccoli, and stir-fry until tender. Return beef to the pan, add oyster sauce, and mix well. Cook until heated through.

Frittata with Veggies

Ingredients:

- 6 eggs
- 1/2 cup milk
- 1 cup mixed vegetables (spinach, bell peppers, onions)
- 1/2 cup shredded cheese
- Salt and pepper to taste

Instructions:

1. **Preheat Oven:** Preheat oven to 375°F (190°C).
2. **Mix Eggs:** In a bowl, whisk together eggs, milk, salt, and pepper. Stir in vegetables and cheese.
3. **Bake:** Pour into a greased oven-safe skillet and bake for 20-25 minutes until set and golden on top.

Spinach and Feta Rice

Ingredients:

- 1 cup cooked rice
- 2 cups fresh spinach (chopped)
- 1/2 cup feta cheese (crumbled)
- 1 tablespoon olive oil
- 1 garlic clove (minced)
- Salt and pepper to taste

Instructions:

1. **Sauté Spinach:** In a pan, heat olive oil and sauté garlic until fragrant. Add spinach and cook until wilted.
2. **Combine:** Stir in cooked rice and feta cheese. Season with salt and pepper, and cook until heated through.

Raspberry Almond Mug Cake

Ingredients:

- 4 tablespoons flour
- 2 tablespoons sugar
- 1/4 teaspoon baking powder
- 1 tablespoon almond extract
- 3 tablespoons milk
- 1 tablespoon vegetable oil
- 2 tablespoons raspberries (fresh or frozen)

Instructions:

1. **Mix Dry Ingredients:** In a microwave-safe mug, combine flour, sugar, and baking powder.
2. **Add Wet Ingredients:** Stir in almond extract, milk, and vegetable oil until smooth. Gently fold in raspberries.
3. **Microwave:** Cook for about 1-1.5 minutes until the cake rises and is cooked through. Let cool slightly before enjoying.

Nacho Cheese Dip

Ingredients:

- 1 cup shredded cheese (cheddar or Mexican blend)
- 1/2 cup cream cheese
- 1/4 cup milk
- 1/4 cup salsa
- Jalapeños (optional)

Instructions:

1. **Combine Ingredients:** In a microwave-safe bowl, mix shredded cheese, cream cheese, milk, and salsa.
2. **Microwave:** Heat in the microwave in 30-second intervals, stirring in between, until melted and smooth.
3. **Serve:** Enjoy warm with tortilla chips!

Feel free to customize these recipes to your taste! Enjoy!

www.ingramcontent.com/pod-product-compliance
Lightning Source LLC
LaVergne TN
LVHW081341060526
838201LV00055B/2792